A VICTORIAN COUNTRY ALBUM

❧ THE PHOTOGRAPHS OF JOSEPH GALE ❧

by Brian Coe

The Oxford Illustrated Press

© Brian Coe

ISBN 0 946609 64 0

Published by:
The Oxford Illustrated Press Limited, Haynes Publishing Group,
Sparkford, Nr Yeovil, Somerset BA22 7JJ, England.

Haynes Publications Inc., 861 Lawrence Drive, Newbury Park,
California 91320, USA.

Printed in England by:
J.H. Haynes & Co Limited, Sparkford, Nr Yeovil, Somerset.

British Library Cataloguing in Publication Data
Gale, Joseph
A Victorian country album : the
photographs of Joseph Gale.
1. Great Britain.   Social life, 1837–1901
I. Title   II. Coe, Brian, *1930–*
941.081

Library of Congress Catalog Card Number 88-81608

Contents

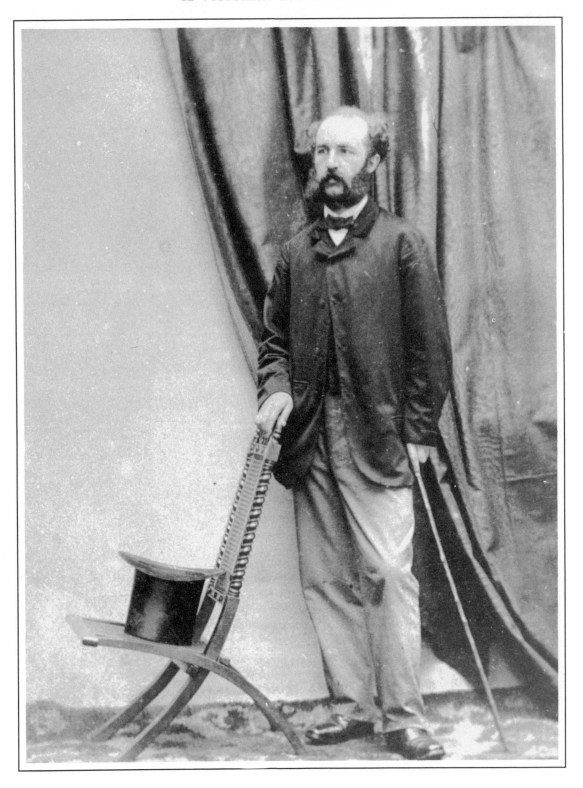

Introduction

Joseph Gale was one of the best known and respected photographers in the last quarter of the nineteenth century, yet he is little known today, relegated, if mentioned at all, to a passing reference in some histories of photography. In part, this is due to the fact that until comparatively recently few of his photographs were thought to have survived. The author, when Curator of the Kodak Museum, then at Harrow, discovered a number of prints which had been made by Kodak Limited in the early years of the century. These had been produced from gelatine dryplate negatives bought from Gale's housekeeper after his death by his friend George Davison, at that time Managing Director of the Company. An exhibition of these prints was staged in 1984 at the Kodak Museum. As a result, contact was made with members of the family, who held substantial numbers of original prints.

Through the generous co-operation of two of Joseph Gale's grand-nieces, Miss Frances Berrill and Mrs Hope Pope, the author, now at the Royal Photographic Society in Bath, was able to arrange in 1986 a second exhibition which attracted great interest, impressing both photographers and non-photographers alike. It is hoped that this book, with the two exhibitions which have preceded it, will help to re-establish the high reputation which Gale had in his lifetime. Gale's chief delight, he said, was in the 'rustic and rural', and his photographs provide a wonderful pictorial record of life in rural England during the last two decades of the nineteenth century. This was a time of great change in the countryside, with the beginnings of mechanisation in agriculture and the increasing influence of the town. Yet old ways still survived in the remoter villages, and Gale sought out and recorded this vanishing scene.

The greater number of the illustrations are from the family collections of Miss Berrill and Mrs Pope, and their generous help and hospitality is most gratefully acknowledged. Lieutenant-Colonel Samuel Pope provided valuable information from family records, and many thanks are due to him. Dr Sadie Ward, of the Museum of English Rural Life at Reading University, provided valuable advice. I am especially indebted to her colleague, the agricultural historian Dr Jonathon Brown, for providing most of the information about nineteenth-century rural life given in the captions to the photographs. I am also indebted to Dr Peter Bowden, archivist of the National Army Museum, for searching out information about Gale's military career. I am glad to thank my colleague Hope Kingsley for her valuable help in reading and commenting on the draft text. Above all, I am grateful to 'Uncle Joe', whose beautiful photographs have been a source of so much pleasure to me during the past eighteen years. I hope that through this book I can repay some of that pleasure by sharing it with a wider public.

Facing page:
Joseph Gale – 1860

CHAPTER ONE

The Early Years

Joseph Gale was born on 16 October, 1830, to John and Sarah Gale. John Gale, a publisher by profession, had married Sarah Hepburn, daughter of a Southwark tanner, on 22 September, 1814, at Bermondsey church. They had three daughters (one died in infancy) and six sons, of whom Joseph was the last. His father died soon after Joseph's birth, on 26 November, 1830, and was buried at Bexley Heath. Joseph was raised in the country, spending much of his early life in Bedford, where he studied art, followed by training at the City of London School as an architect, a profession he followed throughout his life. His vocation and his interest in photography came together in 1890, when, as Honorary Architect to the Camera Club, he designed the new Club House in London's Charing Cross Road. His art training led naturally to an interest in music, poetry and painting, and from an early age he sketched from nature. This skill, combined

'Ye chaysse of ye Swallow tayle'
A self-portrait sketch made by Gale in 1867 to amuse his nephews.

with a great sense of fun, provided endless entertainment for his young nephews and nieces, who were amused by the sketches of 'Uncle Joe' and his adventures. One of his nephews said '(Gale) was a great crony of us boys, caught butterflies with us, boated and bathed and went on long walks with us.' Gale was a great admirer of the painter Turner, and the artist W.B. Leader was a personal friend. These and other influences, including the works of Ruskin, helped to create an interest in the landscape with figures which was to become a major feature of his photographic work.

His working life was spent in London, and he lived in Bermondsey, at 225 Long Lane. He joined the 10th Surrey Rifle Volunteer Corps, based in Bermondsey, at an early age, and was commissioned as an Ensign (equivalent to a 2nd Lieutenant) on 24 February 1864. He was reported to be a crack shot 'at the butts', winning numerous cups and prizes. He was promoted to Lieutenant in 1868, Captain in 1869 and Major in 1881, in which year the Corps was renamed the 3rd Volunteer Battalion, Queen's Royal West Surrey Regiment. He was finally promoted to the honorary rank of Lieutenant Colonel in 1886; his last appearance on the Army List was in January 1891, after which, in his sixties, he presumably retired from active participation in military matters. Interestingly enough, only from then is he referred to in the photographic journals as Lieutenant-Colonel (or Colonel) Gale; during his active service he preferred to be called plain 'Mr'.

Gale (centre) with some of his photographic equipment, including his Ottewill 10 x 8-inch folding camera, in the foreground, c1861.

His first contact with the practice of photography came in 1848, when he was shown the Daguerreotype process by an acquaintance. He took up photography himself in 1859; later he wrote to a friend:

'As a student of architecture I had filled many books with sketches and drawings of buildings of past ages, the delineation of ancient towers and spires (at a period before the wholesale restoration of church architecture) had been the joy of my holidays; but, in an evil moment, the thought possessed me that much might be done, much labour saved, by applying the limited acquaintance I had with photography to the representation of my favourite subjects; and many future holidays saw me in full swing with a 10 inch x 8 inch Ottewill camera and paraphernalia steeple-chasing over a large extent of country.'[1]

When he took up photography, Gale used the wet collodion process which had been developed by Frederick Scott Archer in 1851. This was the first fully practical process for photography on glass plates, which replaced the Calotype process, with its paper negatives, and the Daguerreotype process which gave

Gale with his stereoscopic camera in Jersey, 1861. Note the corner of the portable darktent showing at the side of the building, and the water jugs etc.

unique images on silvered copper plates. In the wet collodion process a carefully cleaned glass plate was coated by hand with a solution of collodion – guncotton dissolved in ether. As soon as the coating had dried to a tacky state it was sensitised by plunging it into a bath of silver nitrate solution. The sensitised plate had to be exposed immediately, before it dried, and then had to be processed at once. This meant that when working away from home a portable darkroom was needed. The photographer had to carry a bulky camera and tripod, glass plates, the portable dark tent, chemicals and even a supply of water if none was to be found on site. In an article in *The Practical Photographer* No. 2 (1903) it was said that in his early years he converted a London cab into a mobile darkroom, with a water cistern on the roof. However, it is likely that most of his early photography was done with the aid of a wheelbarrow darktent which could carry all his apparatus and chemicals, opening up to form a darkroom for sensitising and processing his plates. The Ottewill camera referred to above was an all-wood sliding box pattern camera with hinged folding sides which collapsed flat but opened up to take plates 10 by 12 inches in size. Although this was his favourite model, Gale also used a twin-lens stereoscopic camera, and a Johnson's Pantascopic camera in which a $7^1/_2$ by 12-inch plate was moved by clockwork past an exposing slot in the camera back while the whole camera rotated on the tripod head. This gave a panoramic picture covering a 110-degree angle of view.

The process was not easy to use successfully; Gale later described its problems, and advantages:

'It was a cumbersome business, and the preparation, exposure, and development of the plate – all on the spot – were grave matters, and not to be lightly undertaken. You could not fire off your camera twenty times a day on the chance of hitting once, as with our present facilities we are too much in the habit of doing, but each exposure meant half an hour's careful work under conditions, the delicacy and difficulties of which are unknown – undreamt of in the philosophy of photographers nowadays. The process had its advantages, however, for it enabled one to compare the finished plate with the actual landscape, and to make it express within limits the particular characteristics of the occasion . . .

There can be no doubt that working under these conditions tended to train the faculty of observation, and enabled one readily to decide the capabilities of a subject, and to know whether it possessed the various qualities of a picture . . . figures, even in those days, were my ambition – an ambition thwarted by the conditions under which we worked. For how could any one ensure that a child should not move during an exposure of many seconds, or that a cow should not walk straight out of the picture?'[2]

His earliest photographs, to judge from the small number that have survived, were mainly records of family and of places visited. His interest in the countryside, its people and its wildlife led him to join in 1866 the Amateur Photographic Field Club. Formed in 1858, the Club's members shared a common interest in 'mead and stream' and photography. For many years the Club operated without rules or minute-books, and the membership was limited to 25 only. It was predominantly a social group, without the academic pretensions of other photographic societies. Gale was an enthusiastic member up to his death in 1906. Gale was a keen naturalist (and an expert fly fisherman), with an extensive knowledge of plants and wild life, and although he worked in London for much of his life, most of his leisure time was spent in the country. His friend, the photographer George Davison, wrote in *Sun Artists:*

'Mr. Gale, starting with country associations, has kept the country about him in the town. Of Surrey he has trod every lane; in many a Berkshire cottage of wattle and daub and thatch he is known and welcome. The Sussex Downs, where he takes up summer quarters are, in his own fanciful expression, 'his back garden'. Here he knows every combe in the hills; and many a shepherd's home contains on the walls interesting photographic studies, in which the proud possessor figures as a part.'[3]

Today's photographers, with autofocus cameras, high-speed films and motor drives, can have little understanding of the trials and tribulations of early photographers like Gale. Apart from the technical problems of making the photograph, which were considerable, the photographer had to cope with a further difficulty – the unfamiliarity of the camera to the rural inhabitants of remote villages, at a time barely twenty years after the invention of photography. Gale's own reminiscences are worth quoting at length for the amusing insight they give on this situation:

'*Burying the Baby* – A good many years ago I drove with a friend, well known in the locality, to a village in Buckinghamshire, the same where the inhabitants run down to a pond at the bottom of the village to ascertain if it is raining.

'I wanted to photograph the church, so

stopping at the gate of the churchyard, I proceeded to open out a 10 inch x 8 inch Ottewill camera with long focus landscape lens, and, covering it with a large square of the orthodox black velvet, I slowly carried it on my shoulder to the other side of the churchyard and planted it in position for a view of the church. As I went I had noticed three children watching my movements at a respectful distance, and having put the camera in position I returned in the hope of getting them to sit in my picture, but to my astonishment they were gone. So I went on without them; the plate was inserted, the velvet carefully folded back and the lens cap taken off, and we sat down to time the exposure and await the result.

'Suddenly our quiet chat was broken in upon by three men rushing up in hot haste – the clerk, the sexton, and the gravedigger. A look of blank amazement spread over the face of each one of them when they recognised my friend.

'While two of them remained to interrogate us as to the nature of the dreadful work we were engaged upon, the third went to make examination of my camera; he lifted the velvet, and his suspicions being apparently confirmed, he proceeded to look into the lens to see what he could find; being none the wiser, however, and having succeeded in nothing but spoiling my picture, he returned to his comrades and they then explained to us that they had hurried there in consequence of three children running down to the village to report that "there were two gentlemen in the churchyard *burying a baby*".[4]

Another churchyard adventure occurred when Gale was using the tannin process, which allowed plates to be prepared in advance of the exposure and used dry, but which was also very slow and thus best suited to architecture:

'In order to change the plates, I used a black bag shaped like a balloon into which I put my head and arms, and then fastened the bottom round my waist with an elastic belt; it was provided with armholes and had a round

piece of yellow cloth for a window. I used to take my box of 10 inch x 8 inch plates in with me and the one carrier, and so could change them on my lap easily enough.

'One day I was comfortably seated changing plates with my back to the wall of Elstow churchyard, and was conscious, from the subdued voices of numerous youngsters, that I was an object of interest to a group of juvenile spectators.

'It happened that I had omitted to bring in with me some requisite (a dusting brush or something of the kind), but knowing exactly where I had placed it I thought I could put my hand on it without emerging from my chrysalis covering; so, rising from my seat and passing my hands through the armholes, I groped about with outstretched hands in search of the missing article.

'As I moved the excitement outside increased; first a scream, then a yell, then a general rush in the direction of the village.

'When I quitted my changing bag a few minutes later, not a trace of my group of spectators was left, which was disappointing, as I had meant to induce one or two of them to sit in my picture for the requisite five or ten minutes.

'However, I proceeded with the work of photographing the church, and presently observed my young friends peeping cautiously over the wall, accompanied by a number of grown up people all furnished with sticks and staves. After a hurried glance among the tombstones from behind the wall, the grown up party entered the churchyard. With wild looks and gestures they gazed at me and my camera, and then continued their search for something of which I was ignorant.

'Being evidently unsuccessful they returned to me and asked if I had seen anything; I replied that I could not say that I had not, but what sort of thing? Confusion seemed to possess them: at length one of the party, blushing crimson, asked me in a hesitating manner if I had seen anything like – like a ghost? The children had run down to the village, he said, and frantically declared they had seen a ghost with one eye – with one large yellow eye.

'I would fain have kept a grave face and have carried them on, but was seized with an uncontrollable fit of laughter. When I recovered I explained that I was the ghost, a solid flesh and blood one, however, and presented my arm that they might judge for themselves. But they were difficult to convince, and it was not till I took them to my changing bag, and having attired myself in it, moved about with the appropriate gestures, that they were satisfied that there was not lurking about among the tombstones a black ghost with a large yellow eye.'[5]

If the reader should be surprised at Gale's reference to an exposure of 'five or ten minutes' it should be said that much longer exposures were sometimes needed, as the following story shows:

'*A Scare* – I once paid a visit to a certain island off the west coast of Scotland, and the first morning after my arrival I was out betimes. In the course of wandering up a retired glen I came upon a charming waterfall, and forthwith setting up my 10 inch x 8 inch camera for a view of it, started the exposure of a slow tannin plate. It was now breakfast time, and the exposure would last well on towards dinner, so back to my quarters I must go. I had noticed, however, that the inhabitants of a cottage close by the point of view, but behind it, were watching my movements with much interest, so I called in and asked if they would see that the camera was not disturbed in my absence. As it is not always easy to get a direct answer from a Scotch peasant, I took their consent for granted and hied me back to breakfast a mile or two away.

'. . . After an interval of an hour or so I returned and found the camera just as I had left it; but wishing to be satisfied that nobody had touched it I went to the cottage again. Very tardily, in answer to my knocking, the door of the cottage was opened by a woman, whose

A waterfall on the Isle of Arran, the subject of one of Gale's anecdotes, early 1860s.

terrified looks were only exceeded by those of a man behind her, and of several others behind him.

'On intimating my supposition that nobody had disturbed my camera, the woman responded, "Inteed, sir, no whateffer! we tared na' gang out to look." The man choking with consternation and still half-hiding behind the woman, implored me to tell him what the machine outside was.

'On my telling him that it was a camera and perfectly harmless, he affected to be intimately acquainted with such things, and to regard them with great unconcern, and he even expressed a determination to go and look at the thing for himself; but from this valiant resolve he was turned by the entreaties of the women. He was so desperate, however, as to accompany me, though it must be confessed that he was inclined to regard me (as formerly he had his wife) as a very good shield; and from his earnest inquiries as to the nature of the projectiles and explosives used in the machine, it was evident that his bold demeanour was but the cloak to a most penetrating terror.'[6]

Before leaving Gale's reminiscences, it is worth quoting one more anecdote, not so much for its photographic significance as for the light it throws upon the state of the ecumenical movement in the last century:

'*Little Wesleyans* – A drive of some miles had brought me on one occasion to a certain village, and the camera was duly planted in the centre of the village for a view of the church.

A happy lot of children watched the operation, and the nicest and most suitable were selected to form a group in the foreground of the picture.

'It was soon known throughout the village that there was "someone drawrin the church", and numerous were the visitors. Among the most interested was, of course, the parson, who arrived on the scene as I was finishing and examining the negative, and whose eagerness to see what I had been doing I indulged.

'He looked at the negative and its pretty group with great admiration, which to my astonishment suddenly faded from his face as he exclaimed, "Oh! you have spoiled your picture, you have spoiled your picture, they are all nasty little Wesleyans".'[7]

References

1. *Sun Artists* No. 1, Kegan Paul 1889 p4
2. *Journal of the Camera Club* June 1889
3. *Sun Artists* p4
4. Ibid p5
5. Ibid p6
6. Ibid p7
7. Ibid p5

CHAPTER TWO

Photographic Fame

Gale's early photography had supported his interest in architecture, but more and more the photography of the countryside and its inhabitants became his preoccupation. In the early 1870s, probably through his contacts with other photographers in the Amateur Photographic Field Club, Gale decided to become more involved in the photographic world. In 1874 he entered photographs for selection for the Annual Exhibition of the Photographic Society of Great Britain (later to become the Royal Photographic Society). A series of nineteen views 'Early Rambles with the Field Club' and 'Views of "The Mote", Ightham, Kent' were exhibited. *Photographic News* reported:

'Mr. Gale's reminiscences of rambles with the Field Clubs (sic) contain many charming little bits.'[1]

Gale applied for membership of the Society, and was elected in December 1874; he remained an active member until his death. For the next few years none of his pictures were shown in the annual exhibition, whether through failure to enter or non-selection is not certain, although the former is the most likely explanation.

By 1879, when his pictures were next shown, a major change was under way in photography. In 1871, a London physician, Dr Richard Leach Maddox, had proposed the use of gelatine to replace collodion. The advantage of Maddox's process, in which an emulsion of silver salts in a gelatine solution was coated on a plate and dried, was that the dry plate could be kept for long periods without losing its sensitivity. Although as first published the process was not very much faster than the wet collodion process, improvements in the manufacture of the emulsion, notably the discovery that prolonged heating of the emulsion before coating 'ripened' it, greatly increasing its sensitivity made it eminently practical by 1879. A further advantage for the photographer was that since the plates could be kept for a long period before exposure, commercial manufacture was possible, relieving the photographer of the need to coat plates on the spot, thus making the portable darktent unnecessary. This combination of convenience and high speed, which made 'instantaneous', action-stopping exposures possible, transformed photography. Gale tried out the new plates, and most of his pictures chosen for exhibition in the Photographic Society's 1879 exhibition were on dry plates, mostly made by Wratten and Wainwright.

One of the 1879 pictures was captioned:

'The swallow, too, is come at last,

* * * * *

I saw her dash with rapid wing,

And hailed her as she passed.'

This picture caused a sensation. *The British Journal of Photography* said:

'(Gale's) picture . . . in which a swallow is "caught" on the wing, is a remarkable specimen of instantaneous work. Such subjects have been attempted before, and "seascapes"

'Brixham Trawlers': Gale's first medal-winning picture, in the Photographic Society Exhibition, 1879.

have been by no means uncommon in which birds have been represented in the act of flight; but where such effects have been *bona fide,* and not produced by double printing, the extremely favourable conditions of illumination should be taken into consideration to account for the brevity of the exposure. Here we have a not over-well lit landscape, consisting of foliage mostly in deep shadow overhanging a pool of water, over the surface of which a swallow is dashing "with rapid wing", and both the bird itself and its reflection are perfectly sharp. This result, we are assured both by Mr. Gale himself and others who were present when the picture was taken, is produced by no trick or dodge, but is simply a *bona fide* instantaneous photograph.'[2]

Such was the novelty of an instantaneous exposure short enough to freeze the action of a bird on the wing that doubts were expressed by some about its genuineness. No such reservations were held about the two prints 'Brixham Trawlers', for which he was awarded a medal 'for artistic perfection'. They attracted comments from the press such as 'highly meritorious', 'Simply delicious', 'The softness and delicacy . . . could scarcely be surpassed . . . a truthfulness seldom seen in a photograph' and 'Small in size, they are perfect in composition and technique'. Significantly, most of the other pictures exhibited by Gale at this exhibition were the 'cottage studies' and scenes

'Red Deer in Winter' Gale won a medal for this photograph in the Photographic Society Exhibition in 1881.

of country life of which he was to become the acknowledged master and which the new, faster dry plates with their short exposures now made easy.

From this year, 1879, on, Gale became a regular exhibitor at the Photographic Society's annual exhibition. In the 1880 exhibition, many of his entries were photographs taken in Brittany and Normandy, one of the few occasions when he departed from his beloved English rural scene. Even so, several entries were of local scenes. Several reviewers expressed the opinion that he would have been awarded a medal for his French pictures had he not been one of the judges. It is significant that, with only two previous exhibitions behind

him, he should have been chosen as a judge by the Society. The following year his photographs were eligible for competition, and he was awarded a medal for his 'Red Deer in Winter'. *The Photographic News* said:

'Mr. Gale's masterpiece, according to the judges, is a tiny winter sketch (104) – a deer park in the snow and rime. Two magnificent trees are in the foreground; their solid black trunks, in delightful contrast with the delicate twigs all encrusted with silvery frost, are exquisitely limned . . . The red deer in the distance impart life to a marvellously good bit of photography.'[3]

Gale was among the medal winners at the Society's exhibition the following year, with one of his series of West Country pictures 'A Doorway Group: St. Ives, Cornwall'. 'A more perfect composition we have seldom seen rendered by photographic means' said *The British Journal of Photography*.[4]

Several reviewers noted that this year he had included groups of people in his Cornish pictures. This was to become the pattern from now on.

Gale's pictures now became a standard feature of the Photographic Society's Annual Exhibition. In the 1884 Exhibition he received a medal for a Lantern Transparency. He had become a master of slide making for the magic lantern, a specialised process neglected by many photographers, but capable of yielding most beautiful results when well done. The following year he was once again a judge of the Exhibition, missing a medal for his work in consequence. *The British Journal of Photography* said 'the figure studies are even better than usual'.[5] Two of Gale's pictures were supplied as illustrations in the Photographic Society's Journal in 1885; one, a scene of a team returning from ploughing was reproduced as a Woodburytype, the other, 'The Sand Pit', was illustrated by photoengraving. In 1886, for the first time in a number of years, none of Gale's photographs were shown at the Society's Annual Exhibition. He seems to have been concentrating on lantern slide making; some of his very best work was selected by the Camera Club for an exchange with the Society of Amateur Photographers of New York in May

1886. In December of that year, some of his slides were shown at a lantern meeting at the Camera Club, whose Journal reported 'The greatest pleasure of the evening was derived from a set of Mr. Gale's pictures . . .'[6] At another Camera Club meeting in February 1887 his slides were acclaimed, especially 'a fine study of barges on the river at Blackfriars Bridge after a snowstorm, in which the result was most artistic, the atmosphere being perfect'.[7] More slides were shown at the Camera Club in March and June, and in May at the North Surrey Photographic Society, when they were described as 'exquisite' in *The Photographic News*.[8] In the Photographic Society's Exhibition of that year his lantern slides were awarded a medal, but among his photographic prints in that show was one which was to become the best-known of all his photographs.

References

1. *The Photographic News* 23 October 1874
2. *The British Journal of Photography* 10 October 1879
3. *P.N.* 14th October 1881
4. *B.J.P.* 13 October 1882
5. *B.J.P.* 16th October 1885
6. *Journal of the Camera Club* 10th January 1887
7. *P.N.* 25 February 1887
8. *P.N.* 27 May 1887

CHAPTER THREE

Sleepy Hollow and After

In May 1887, Gale went on a Camera Club outing to Gomshall, in Surrey. At Crossway's Farm, Abinger, he took what was to become his most famous photograph, 'Sleepy Hollow'. *The Amateur Photographer* described it as:

'The idyll of "Sleepy Hollow," two horses lazily sucking-in the crystal stream from a babbling brook, whilst their driver looks on in a *dolce far niente* attitude. All the lines of the picture, the motionless trees, the light fleecy clouds, give the idea of repose and rest'.[1]

In an illustrated article by H.P. Robinson in *The Amateur Photographer*, he described 'Sleepy Hollow' as:

'A beautiful example of balance, both of lines and tones, as well as of expression . . . Mr. Gale, in his little pictures, always contrives to show how much art can be packed into a small space.

'I will leave the student to find out for himself how beautiful are the lines of the composition, merely suggesting that he should try to imagine any part of the composition left out, even to the stone and post in the water, and the dark arch under the bridge, and he will immediately feel the want of it. As to the tone, let him take away the man and horses, and what becomes of the rest? It is a pretty scene, but without the figures would have no particular interest. The black of the horses by contrast puts atmosphere into the whole of the picture, and makes every bit of it valuable'.[2]

'Sleepy Hollow' was shown first at the Photographic Society's annual exhibition in October 1887. Although it did not win a medal,

it was much commended. *The Amateur Photographer* said:

' "Sleepy Hollow" we commend especially . . . There is a finish . . . and a careful attention to detail which it would be well for so many amateurs (those of the slap-dash species) to seriously study and try to profit by.'[3]

'Sleepy Hollow' was included in a series of six photographs which won the *Amateur Photographer* silver medal at the Liverpool Amateur Photographic Association's exhibition in March 1888, and also took the Association's gold medal for best landscape work. In this exhibition, for the first time, Gale forsook albumen paper for platinotype printing, which he was to adopt almost universally from this time on. In November 1888, the picture won the gold medal at the Oldham Exhibition, in the Champion class, for pictures which had already taken prizes, open to both amateurs and professionals.

When the publishers Kegan Paul chose Gale's work for the first of a series of portfolios of high quality photogravure reproductions of photographs, 'Sleepy Hollow' was one of the four pictures selected (the others were 'Brixham Trawlers', 'A Foggy Day on the Thames' and 'Homeward from Plough'). Gale's friend and leading pictorial photographer George Davison wrote the commentary. The Autotype Company, manufacturers of carbon printing materials, used it as the frontispiece to their book *ABC Guide to Autotype Prints* in 1893, and also included it in an album of Gale's photographs which they published in the same year. In 1897, a large photomechanical repro-

duction of 'Sleepy Hollow' was distributed widely in the north of England as a Christmas gift from traders.

The great popular success of 'Sleepy Hollow' was matched by his considerable reputation among photographers. He was in great demand as a judge of photographic competitions and exhibitions, and in February 1888 he was elected to the Council of the Photographic Society of Great Britain. In May of that year he was made President of the newly-formed West Surrey Amateur Photographic Association (with his friend George Davison as Vice-President). His work continued to receive recognition; at the Nottingham Photographic Exhibition in February 1888 he won the *Amateur Photographer* silver medal for his print 'Little Chippers', as well as a bronze medal for a series of landscapes. Several of his pictures were shown in the Crystal Palace Photographic Exhibition in February 1888, *The Amateur Photographer* said 'There is certainly nothing in the exhibition equal to these in the same class of work'.[4] His entries in the Photographic Society's Annual Exhibition received much acclaim 'a fine series of pictures . . . unsurpassed in their beauty of tone and truth of aerial effect' *(Saturday Review); '*they are gems, and perfect in technique' *(Amateur Photographer)*. He was very popular with his fellow photographers, who regarded him with respect and affection. *The British Journal of Photography,* reporting on the Camera Club Conference in April 1888, broke into lyrical prose:

'At times the door will open gently, and a zephyr, a balmy Gale, will steal in and refresh the presentees with his latest sylvan inspiration, while the joint secretaries murmur in harmony,

"Blow, gently Gale, and on your wing
Your latest, sweetest picture bring"[5]

His lantern slides continued to attract praise. The Society of Amateur Photographers of New York were impressed with his 'superb' slides sent as part of the exchange set in 1887; more of his slides were included in a further exchange in December 1888. At the North Surrey Photographic Society meeting in January 1889 a lantern slide show concluded 'with a splendid collection by Mr. J. Gale. The audience . . . applauded again and again as Mr. Gale's slides were thrown upon the screen.'[6]

1889 brought more success; the *Amateur Photographer* silver medal for the best picture at the Richmond Photographic Society Exhibition in January was awarded for his picture 'Home from the Plough', and the Society's silver medal was given for a series of four pictures. *The Photographic News* said:

'No one will be astonished that Mr. Gale has carried off two awards. The mantle of Mr. Manners Gordon has worthily fallen on him. But, besides the little landscape views, in which he so closely resembles the distinguished wet plate worker first mentioned, the possibilities of modern methods have enabled him to produce rustic scenes that at the moment are almost unique. "Almost" is the right word to use, for he may be regarded as the founder of a modern school and some of the most successful pictures in the exhibition under notice clearly demonstrate that he has many admirers among the amateurs'.[7]

He was given a one-man show at the Camera Club in May 1889, with more than a hundred pictures displayed. *The Amateur Photographer* said 'Most of them are gems of the first water, and exhibit that attention to picturesque detail for which this artist's pictures are remarkable'.[8]

A highlight of 1889 was the publication of the first issue of *Sun Artists*, mentioned earlier. *The British Journal of Photography* said of it:

Facing page:
'Sleepy Hollow': Exhibited first at the Photographic Society Exhibition in 1887, and subsequently shown at many other exhibitions and in several publications. (Taken in May, 1887, at Crossways Farm, Abinger, in Surrey, this is Gale's best-known photograph.)

'The projectors have acted most wisely in the selection of the artist by whose works this number is illustrated. Mr. Joseph Gale ranks, and for many years has ranked, among the very foremost of those whose artistic taste and manipulative skill have conduced to elevate photographs from scientific facsimiles of nature into the realm of art.'[9]

Thirty-two of his pictures were shown in an exhibition by members of the Amateur Photographic Field Club at the Camera Club in February 1890; they included some of his early work with the Pantascopic panoramic camera. He continued as a Photographic Society Council member, and as a regular judge at the Annual Exhibition, where he continued to exhibit his pictures. He found time to lead, with his friend George Davison, a three-day Camera Club excursion to Arundel and Amberley in September 1890. A light-hearted report over the pseudonym 'Ernest Humphrey' reported in the *Journal of the Camera Club* that the party: 'left London Bridge for Arundel by the five o'clock train, including Mr. Urbanity [George Davison], of Her Majesty's Civil Service – in which he holds the office of Lord High Purse Bearer; [and] Mr. Tempest [Gale], whose charming studies of sheep and Sussex scenery are so much admired by all those who visit the Photographic Exhibitions . . .

'Breakfast [at the Norfolk Hotel] at half-past eight; and being on artistic work intent, of course a very light meal was all we dared indulge in; this consisted of mutton cutlets, about six pounds of steak, kidneys and bacon, stewed tomatoes, poached eggs, and more bacon, &c.; but the soul of Signor Romano was disquieted because there was no omelette to follow this too meagre fare; however, with the help of jams of sorts and marmalade, he managed to stave off the pangs of hunger. Shortly after this our wagonette drew up to the door, and was quickly loaded with cameras, tripods, and other impedimenta, enough to fill a small wagon . . .'

Later during the weekend, the party (of

A study of sheep, photographed on the Camera Club outing to Arundel in September 1890, as described by 'Ernest Humphery'.

eight!) was treated to a demonstration by Gale on photographing sheep:

'. . . suddenly I saw Mr. Tempest coming through the bushes, armed with his camera; and then I learnt for the first time what are the proper methods to adopt for photographing sheep. First he talked to them, then he sang sweet songs, till the sheep fancied that Orpheus with his lute had come back again . . . Anyhow, the sheep were quite enchanted at the lovely sounds, and grouped themselves in poetic attitudes of rapt attention; and then, as they came too close, I was ordered to creep on all-fours towards them, and bark.'[10].

Clearly, everyone had fun!

At this time an upheaval was taking place in the photographic world. A controversy had developed in the Photographic Society over the action of the Honorary Secretary in removing a number of prints by George Davison from the Exhibition in 1891 on the grounds that they had been entered late. Furthermore, an argument arose with the grand old man of English photography, H.P. Robinson, over his presence during the hanging of the Exhibition, at which Robinson, as a vice-president, believed he was entitled to be present. As a result, Robinson, Davison and others left the Society. The first result of this break-away was an invitation exhibition at the Camera Club in October 1892, with pictures selected for their artistic merit, and with no competitive element or medals. Gale, who was on the hanging committee for the new show had six pictures displayed – 'which are, we need hardly say, perfect in technique' said *The Photographic News*.[11] However, he had not left the Society, and, indeed, gained a medal for a series of seven pictures in the Annual Exhibition in September 1892. As *The Photographic News* said 'A photographic exhibition at Pall Mall, in which Col. Gale was not the recipient of a medal,

A caricature by 'f/64' from *The Amateur Photographer*, 12 October, 1894, reporting on the Salon exhibition. 'There was also a well-known photographer present whom I always connect with Southdown mutton in a strong wind.'

would be an anachronism, for from his camera has come some of the finest photographs ever produced.'[12]

The break-away group formed The Linked Ring, a brotherhood of photographers devoted to excellence in photography. Many of the Links, as the members were called, were devotees of the new Impressionistic school of photography, led by George Davison, in which diffusion of focus and special printing processes were used to subdue detail. But there was room in the Ring for the traditional 'f/64' man with his finely detailed images, of which Gale was the greatest exponent. Gale was elected at the first meeting on 27 May 1982, and took the Link name of 'Rambler' (all members had a pseudonym). From then on he regularly exhibited at the Salon, the Ring's annual show, as well as at the (now) Royal Photographic Society's Annual Exhibition. Gale continued as a judge for the Exhibition, and a member of the Society's Council until 1897.

Gale was awarded another one-man show, of nearly one hundred prints, at the Camera Club in January 1896, which attracted, as always, favourable comment:

'As to Colonel Gale's work, everyone who knows anything of pictorial photography knows the high excellence of his work. The writer once heard a remark somewhat to this effect, "It really would be quite a treat if Gale would show us a failure. Every negative is so exactly timed, never over or under exposed or developed. Every print so faultless and clean, etc., etc., etc., "'[13]

'Then, the care and attention he gives to the technique of his art, the accurate focussing and definition, the correctness of exposure, and the conscientiousness of his printing – are not these so many object-lessons to the young photographer in danger of being persuaded that the cultivation of photographic art is bound up with diffusion of focus and other fads?'[14]

Despite his advancing years – he was now in his later sixties – he was still busy as an exhibition judge, much in demand by

The panel of judges for the 1902 Royal Photographic Society Annual Exhibition, the last at which Gale was a judge. From left to right, standing: Chapman Jones, W.R. Bland, J.C.S. Mummery, Lt. Colonel Joseph Gale. Seated: E. Sanger Shepherd, William Crooke, Dr. P.H. Emerson, Sir William Abney.

photographic societies. Despite an accident which left him on crutches, he managed to be present at the October 1896 soirée of the Royal Photographic Society's Exhibition, of which he had been a judge, and in which, as usual, he had several pictures hung. Probably because of his health, the following year he withdrew from election to the RPS Council, and for the first time for many years was not a judge of the Exhibition. He did manage to send three pictures to the Salon, however. The after-effects of his illness curtailed his photography for a time, but in 1898 he had recovered, and was able to send sixty-two prints to the major Crystal Palace Exhibition in 1898, organised by the Royal Photographic Society. They were shown with a bay to themselves; *The Amateur Photographer* remarked 'Col. Gale's work stands alone, and may be said to have marked an epoch, and even set a school'.[15] *The Photographic News* said 'truly a wondrous show . . . Colonel Gale has, indeed, been one of the pioneers of artistic photography, "individualised" in the extreme, and certainly one of the five leaders of the present day. We cannot speak higher of such splendid examples'.[16]

He resumed his judging activities for the Royal Photographic Society, continuing in this role until 1902, although he no longer entered pictures. He was able to present a Lantern Evening at the Society in December 1900, showing a hundred slides of a very wide range of rural subjects. 'Almost every slide was a perfect picture, and effectually controverted the assertion which has sometimes been made that an artistic lantern slide was an impossibility . . . Several of the slides were representations of scenes which no longer exist; for, as he remarked of one of them "I took it last year – this year the County Council have taken it."'[17] In March 1901 sixty of his photographs were given a House Exhibition at the Society's headquarters, and he spoke at the opening.

In February 1902, he was elected an Honorary Fellow of the Royal Photographic Society in recognition of his lay service to photography. But he was now threatened with eye trouble, which necessitated a double operation, prompting a sympathetic response from the photographic press:

'We sincerely hope that with surgical aid and opticians' help Col. Gale will, without trouble, give the world much more of his dainty photography, and be as frequent as ever in those photographic circles where, it is not too much to say, he is personally beloved as well as respected.'[18]

Fortunately, things went well, and The Amateur Photographer was able to report in August 1902:

'It was . . . with real delight that we met Col. Gale last week far better than one could have hoped to find him so soon after such a trying ordeal. The trouble with his sight appears cured and convalescence almost complete.'[19]

He was (for the last time) a judge at the Royal Photographic Society's Annual Exhibition in 1902, and was able to enter a picture for the Salon that year, 'Chairs to mend, Umbrellas to mend!'. Reviewing that exhibition, George Bernard Shaw said of it 'The most thoroughgoing example of the old school, Lieutenant-Colonel Gale's "Chairs to Mend; Umbrellas to Mend" staggers humanity at the Salon . . . Robust and barbarious, it is not at all put out of countenance by the Steichens and Demachys, being as successful in its way as they are in theirs.'[20]

In 1903, for the last time, he showed prints at the Royal Photographic Society Annual Exhibition, in the Invitation Section. A portrait of him was reproduced in the August 1903 issue of The Photographic Journal, celebrating the Society's fiftieth anniversary. His last exhibition success came with the award of a bronze medal in the St Louis Exhibition in America in the Autum of 1904.

With the progressive loss of eyesight he had to give up active participation in the affairs of photography, but he continued both to take photographs and to encourage others. He attended a meeting of the Amateur Photographic Field Club on 23 June 1906 'not, it is true, with his camera, but what was more wonderful, he posed figures for his younger and less experienced members, and gave advice as to composition, etc.'[21] On 6 August 1906, just after midnight, he died 'from an internal trouble that had long been threatening'[22] The Amateur Photographer, in its obituary notice, spoke for the photographic world:

'He will be missed, and more than missed; we think of him now, and shall always recollect him, with real affection, and as a result of intimate personal acquaintance remember him with respect as one of the best of the old "school".'[23]

He was buried at Norwood, where lay also his mother and four brothers and sisters. He had never married, and left most of his effects to his housekeeper. His friend, George Davison, who at that time was Managing Director of Kodak Limited, acquired from her Gale's dry-plate negatives, which were used for some years to make specimen prints for the Company. The negatives did not survive the years, but many of the prints did, and they are held in the Kodak Museum, now at the National Museum of Photography, Film and Television in Bradford. Other work by Gale is in the Collection of the Royal Photographic Society in Bath, as well as in the possession of the family. They provide a lasting memorial to one of the masters of photography of the later nineteenth century.

References

1. *Amateur Photographer* 9 March 1888
2. *A.P.* 31 May 1889
3. *A.P.* 21 October 1887
4. *A.P.* 9 March 1888
5. *British Journal of Photography* 27 April 1888
6. *A.P.* 11 January 1889
7. *The Photographic News* 18 January 1889
8. *A.P.* 7 June 1889
9. *B.J.P.* 1 November 1887
10. *Journal of the Camera Club* October 1890
11. *P.N.* 21 October 1892
12. *P.N.* 30 September 1892
13. *A.P.* 31 January 1896
14. *B.J.P.* 31 January 1896
15. *A.P.* 29 April 1898
16. *P.N.* 6 May 1898
17. *B.J.P.* 7 December 1900
18. *A.P.* 20 February 1902
19. *A.P.* 7 August 1902
20. *A.P.* 16 October 1902
21. *A.P.* 21 August 1906
22. *A.P.* 21 August 1906
23. *A.P.* 14 August 1906

CHAPTER FOUR

Gale's Photography

George Davison, writing in the introduction to *Sun Artists,* described the characteristics of Gale's photography:

'There would be little difficulty in any exhibition in putting the finger at once upon pictures produced by Mr. Gale. They are marked by a delicacy of detail, precision in line composition, careful exclusion of anything awkward and inharmonious, a happy introduction of figures, and success in the combination of clouds with landscapes from different negatives . . . Mr. Gale's special delight, as he has himself said, has been in the rustic and rural. His work has much of its motive and origin in his keen, never-satisfied love of the country. Country customs and manners have been matters of close and constant observation with him on his occasional summer flights to some peaceful village or hospitable farm . . . It is interesting to notice how observation and knowledge teach tact in dealings with the flock and the herd. Which of us would be diverted from a serious intent to picture sheep by a friendly desire to amuse the woolly ones by bowling a hat (his own) in such a manner as to bring around it the whole company of silly curious things, staring at the shapely felt with wonder and amaze? . . . How important to a photographer tact and judgement are in dealing with the various contingencies which arise in the study of figure in landscape work, every man with experience will know. Some meet the circumstance with a cheery 'known-you-all-my-life' advance, and this is all well if there is no tinge of condescension in the introduction; others of an older school naturally drop into a more courtly demeanour, having flavour of bygone days in their approaches and dealings with models, or the 'landed proprietors' with whom the prosecution of their hobby brings them into contact. Mr Gale is the type of this latter class and very rarely has had to put up with a rebuff.'[2]

It would not be possible to better this account of Gale's philosophy of photography. His success with arranging figures in his landscapes and 'cottage studies' was due to his kindly and courteous approach to potential models. He described how he approached a typical subject in his paper 'Out with a Camera – Choosing Subjects', read to the Camera Club in 1888:

'Here is a cottage – one of many in the village – very pretty, very nice, with the doorway partly overgrown with vine, and some worn red brick steps leading up to it, and a latticed window abutting on it. One would not think of taking that as it is; but what a capital setting for a group! Let us knock at the door and ask the occupier if we may take a 'sketch' of her pretty doorway (if we were to call it 'a photograph' she might mistake us for itinerant professionals, and expect to be asked some day for payment – such things have happened). It maybe she is a comfortable and obliging sort of woman, and would not mind our asking her to stand in the doorway with a broom in her hand and one or two of those fair-haired children seated on the step, perhaps with their dolls or their school slate. Yes! she is pleased with the thought of it; she won't mind if you ask her to let you borrow a pail, or a jar,

or a stool, and the bigger girl may come, the other is going to school.

'Now, then, treat the subject as you think best. The woman may be seated, and the girl standing, slate in hand, doing her sums, or standing broom in hand or knitting needles, while the girl prepares to move off with a basket on her arm. There are half-a-dozen ways of treating this doorway and these two figures, open to your fancy; but let it be a simple, natural treatment of the subject, the accessories subservient to the group, and only such as you would be likely to find at the cottage doorway in the ordinary way. Do what you can to make the people feel easy and at home with you; occupy them so that they may think of what you have set them to do, and not of the camera; and be careful not to try your sitters' patience too much. You know the capabilities of your lens, and should know how much will be comprised in your view. Get the focus and the margins of your picture, and then set your models within it where you have made up your mind they will look best and most natural. It ought to be scarcely necessary to focus again, but a last brief look on the ground-glass may be taken, and the plate inserted into the camera. Your figures in position, you may do all the little finishing touches to the hat, the hands, or the attitude – see that the accessories are right; and perhaps you may first practise them in keeping still for two or three seconds, telling them you are not going to take them this time. If they behave as you wish, they will have recovered their breath for the real exposure, for it is sometimes an awful ordeal to them (unless you have done your part nicely and kindly); it will not be so bad the next time. But give them due notice of the real exposure, and due notice

when it is done, for they are grouped, not looking toward the camera, and will think it necessary to keep still until you liberate them. Our sitters have behaved properly, the lighting was good, and everything favourable. One of those silver coins we have taken care to provide ourselves with will be an acceptable present to the little girl; or, just think: with such a negative as this will turn out, it will be well worth a shilling paid to the mother to buy a book, or another doll for the children. But do not promise a copy of the photograph unless you mean conscientiously to fulfil. The promise is treasured up, and the photograph looked forward to anxiously, and great will be the disappointment at its non-arrival, and disrepute of the amateur. Now let us help, or offer to help put back the things in their places, and move on . . .'[2]

The sending of a copy of the photograph to his models was a matter of honour with Gale, and his prints had pride of place in cottages throughout rural England. On one occasion, when he lost the name and address of a West Country fisherman, he stuck a head cut from a print onto the envelope, asking the postmaster of the town to deliver it to the person concerned. The picture duly arrived at the right destination! Those indeed were the days.

Although most of his early photography was done on 10 x 8-inch plates, with the coming of the gelatine dry plate in the late 1870s Gale turned to a smaller format of $7\frac{1}{2}$ x 5 inches. He rarely exhibited anything other than same-size contact prints from the negative, which earned him the epithet of 'chief miniaturist amongst photographers'. His exhibition prints at first were made on albumen paper, plain paper coated with eggwhite and sensitised with silver nitrate, and printed under a negative by the direct action of sunlight. This was the standard medium for printing from the early 1850s, but from 1888 he adopted the platinum process, which gave an image in platinum rather than silver, and most of the surviving prints made by him are in this form

Facing page: **The cottage of Mrs Alf Pearce, at Long Crendon, Buckinghamshire, the photographing of which Gale described in 'Out with a camera – choosing subjects' in 1888.**

(except those made by Kodak Limited after his death, which are on Solio gelatine-silver printing-out paper). Although hand cameras were available from the mid 1880s, and increasingly were used by other photographers, he never forsook his stand camera and the long exposures with small lens apertures which enabled him to record the clarity of detail which characterise his photographs. He had advice for the hand camera user, though:

'In these days of magazine and rapid-firing rifles, one of the important points impressed upon our soldiers is *Fire discipline.*' So with our magazine cameras and rapid-firing apparatus, let us be careful that we reserve our fire until we have something definite to aim at, and never fire unless there is a reasonable probability of hitting.'[3] Very sound advice, even (or especially) today!

Gale had strong views on the scope and the limitations of photography, compared with what the artist could do:

'The painter may conventionalize. By this I mean that he may exercise his inventive faculties for improving Nature . . . He may remove a bar or two from yonder rustic gate, or omit half the pales from the adjoining fence, or place them at any angle that suits his fancy. He may take down the obtrusive branch from the tree in the middle distance that mars his skyline. He may even put a foot-plank across the purling brook that meanders through his landscape and add a handrail if he likes . . . What can the photographer do in this direction? Let him remove that rail from the gate, or take down that obtrusive limb of the tree, and the owner will be down upon him, will run him in before the 'beak', and he will be mulcted in 40s, or a fortnight, with costs, and probably damages.'

' . . . Are we to attempt to make the *lens* conventionalize, because the painter in his necessity *must* do so? Are we to try to blur up the leaves of our trees into a mass without detail, or run the tiles of our roof one into the other, or do away with the distinct line (or limit) of demarcation between one plane and another which exists in Nature, and give it a blurred edge not existing in Nature, because the painter in his necessity, and with his limited appliances and his short span of life in this world, is bound to do so?'[4]

In this statement Gale tackled the controversy which raged in the early 1890s over the impressionistic movement in photography, led by his friend George Davison. The photo-impressionists claimed that by subduing detail the photographer could approach the artist's aim of conveying the immediate impression of a scene, rather than its distracting detail. Gale's view, that of the traditional photographer, was

'Is it not a lesser evil to have one's attention arrested by the beauty of accessory detail than to have constantly to exercise one's inventive genius to discover whether a background is a distant bit of landscape, a brick wall, or a lattice-girder?'[5]

Earlier, he had made the point:

'It is photography we are considering. As the saying is "Let every tub stand on its own bottom", we shall find that photography has a bottom broad and solid enough to stand upon without being propped up by extraneous aids. It has gone through the stages of birth, crawling, toddling, ambling, and has now arrived at the stage of robustness.

'There is some fear of its assuming the strutting stage by apeing (sic) artists and painters and their conventionalities, and otherwise getting outside of its proper and legitimate sphere. Let us, by all means, study how painters achieve success, how they translate nature, how they put soul into their work, and let us do what we can in the same direction consistently with the tools at our command and the many other differing considerations and conditions of our handicraft. Let us not, however, stick feathers about our sombre bird, and call it a peacock!'[6]

Good advice, today as then. However, the argument ran and ran, and was never resolved, but Gale's pictures were the strongest argument for the traditional view.

He was a purist in technique, believing that the photographer's task was to select the subject, arranging it by choice of view and manipulation of movable elements where appropriate, and by choice of time of day ensure that the lighting was the best possible. Once the negative was exposed, that should be the end of manipulation.

'In landscape photography (I mean landscape as distinct from portraiture) hand work in any form on the negative should be considered inadmissible; certainly the less hand work the better. It may be legitimate to spot out defects should such perchance or accident be met with, but the introduction into a picture of features that are not produced by real photography is to be deprecated.

'To manufacture a horse's ear on the negative, or a cow's tail – things often observed to be absent if taken in summer after the month of June – cannot be called photography; but to manufacture *clouds* and palm them off as photography is distinctly reprehensible; it begins with fraud, which will be discovered, it will end in discomfiture of the perpetrator and discredit to photography.

'Perhaps even less allowable should it be considered to touch up prints by paint or other hand work, and introduce features not existing in the negative. We should leave to the sun to pencil . . .'[7]

Gale's exception to this rule was to print-in clouds in his landscapes. The photographic plates in his time were far more sensitive to blue light than any other colour, and the result was usually that an exposure sufficient to record the landscape grossly overexposed the sky, which printed to a featureless white. A separate plate, exposed for the sky alone, might record the clouds if they were present; alternatively, clouds recorded on another occasion might be printed in. This had to be done with some care:

'For instance, in printing sunlight clouds from one negative with sunlit landscape from another negative, we must be careful that the source and direction of lighting for the two correspond, or thereabouts; for we must remember that the lighting of clouds is subject to the same law as the lighting of a landscape or a building.'[8]

Gale was a past master at the selection and printing in of clouds, even on lantern slides, where their small size made the technique quite difficult. Unlike Gale, who carefully collected his cloud negatives whenever the skies presented an opportunity, many photographers bought sets of commercial cloud negatives and made little attempt to match them to their landscapes. On the other hand, Gale once encountered someone with a different problem.

'A gentleman – a stranger – called on me. After a bit of a palaver that he was an amateur photographer, he remarked that he was quite sure I must possess a great many landscape negatives (a fact I could not conscientiously deny); he then went on to say that he had secured some very fine cloud negatives from his top window, but not having leisure to give to outdoor photography he would be very glad if he could come to some arrangement to borrow some of my landscape negatives to print them with!'[9]

It is as well, perhaps, that Gale had a great sense of humour!

Finally, Gale had something to say about the growing practice in his time for photographers to hand over the processing and printing of their negatives to someone else:

'Do only as much as you can complete yourself without extraneous aid. If you are in

Overleaf, left-hand page: **A landscape first printed plain, with a featureless sky, and then printed with a dramatic cloud negative.**

Overleaf, right-hand page: **Two versions of a landscape with different skies.**

love with your art and your subject (and if you are not – *cui bono?)*, you will tenderly and lovingly take a pleasure in completing the work from beginning to end; you will not send the plate to the maker to be developed, and your negative to the professional printer, or your skilful friend, to be printed. To those with whom such a practice is a necessity, I say nothing, except that they must not call the result their own work. But to adopt such a method, and then send the pictures to an exhibition as your work, reminds one irresistibly of one of those miserable mendicants one sees in the public streets – there he sits, cowering on the pavement, alongside of a set of wonderful productions in coloured chalk, craving alms, gulling the passers-by with the belief that he was the talented artist; while the truth is that the real operator has been doing half a dozen others for a like number of similarly helpless wretches, and is now away at the 'Pig and Whistle' enjoying his beefsteak and onions and his pot of "arf and arf".[10]

Again, one must ask, what is new?

References

1. *Sun Artists* pp3-4
2. *The Photographic News* 7 September 1888
3. *Journal of the Camera Club* November 1890
4. *J.C.C.* August 1893
5. *J.C.C.* August 1893
6. *Amateur Photographer* 25 October 1889
7. *A.P.* 28 September 1888
8. Ibid
9. Ibid
10. *J.C.C.* December 1890

The Photographs of Joseph Gale

A COTTAGE STUDY

A well-kept cottage with neat thatch and walls of mixed stone and brick. The lad at the gate is off to school with his bundle of books on a strap over his shoulder.

A BREAK FROM GARDENING

Another tidy cottage, with a garden more in keeping with the modern image of the Victorian country garden. An extensive vegetable plot lies beyond the flower patch. The ubiquitous birdcage hangs by the cottage door.

Water from the Pool

With no well or stream handy, in the days long before universal mains supplies, water was got where it could be found. Here, it is from a small spring by the muddy roadside. The man appears to be off to work, hedging perhaps, with his long-handled hook and saw. In time-honoured fashion, his trousers are tied below the knees with string, perhaps to keep at bay rodents disturbed by his work! The woman in her bonnet carries a wooden bucket with an iron handle.

THE YOUNG OSIER PICKERS

Children enjoying a break from collecting willow stems, used for basket making, and playing beside a small watermill.

AN ENCOUNTER IN THE LANE

*A four-wheeled cart loaded with agricultural baskets.
Probably the basket-maker is delivering his stock, or is
perhaps on his way to market.*

THE OSIER BARGE

Basket willows being loaded onto Perseverance, *owned by W.
Whitehouse & Son, Carriers, of Brentford, operating from
London to Reading. There were several osier beds in the
Reading area, at Twyford, and along the River Kennet
towards Newbury. A somewhat undernourished-looking horse
waits, presumably to pull the barge.*

Water from the Stream, 1889

*For those who lived nearby, the still (comparatively)
unpolluted stream was a convenient source of washing water,
saving a walk to the well. For the children, it was a source of
infinite pleasure.*

Fetching Water

*This communal well seems to be in a street in a small town;
it has a drainage system, at any rate. The miniscule front
garden to the lady's cottage is fenced with barrel staves.*

BACK FROM THE WELL

The picturesque thatch and the weathered turned-wood pillars may look attractive, but this cottage was probably cold and damp, with its floor well below outside ground level, and poor ventilation. Note the line of slates set up at the top of the step down, presumably to deflect rainwater running down the sloping path from entering the house. The galvanised metal pail and the woman's costume show urban influences.

TIME FOR A CHAT

Farm labourers on their way to or from work, with their forks and other tools. The women wear the hooded bonnets which gave good shade when working in the fields. The woman on the left has a crocheted shawl. All carry baskets of one sort or another. The man has a shoulder bag for tools and lunch, the woman in the middle has a small egg basket and a typical shopping basket is on the arm of the woman on the right.

GOING TO MARKET

Two women in their donkey market cart at the edge of town,
passing a tradesman with his delivery cart. The rule of the
road and driving on the left did not seem to matter too much.

A MID-DAY BREAK

Outside 'The Bell Commercial Inn' in a large village or small town, big enough to have gas street lighting, the carter cools his horse off in the pond, a common practice on hot summer days, while others pass the time of day leaning on the wooden drinking trough.

WATER FROM THE BROOK

A young girl in a smart straw hat and dress helps to fill mother's galvanised metal bucket from a small stream.

AT THE STREAM

The young girls wear pinafores, a standard part of their dress in Gales's time. They were easy to make at home, from lengths of cheap cloth bought at the village shop or market town drapers.

'OFF TO MARKET – YOU'LL TAKE CARE OF BABY'
Exhibited at the Photographic Society Exhibition, 1884

An attractive river scene. The British Journal of Photography *said it was 'the best composition of Mr. Gale's, and the picture tells its own story. A rustic cottage, a pebbly brook, and wooden bridge form the groundwork of the subject. The figures are two – mother and daughter – the former of whom calls out as she crosses the bridge the words of the title.'* The Photographic News *said it 'has an air of truth which makes it a good picture.'*

THE WATERMILL
A massive undershot twin-wheel watermill with a delightful collection of additions and extensions in a variety of materials.

FISHING FOR TIDDLERS

The shepherd and his dog inspect the catch of two youngsters fishing in the pool in the meadow. A group of neatly thatched corn ricks stand in the background, caught by the late afternoon sun.

A BREAK FROM HAY-MAKING

Two workers with scythes take a break on a bridge at the edge of the hay-field. A wonderfully atmospheric summer landscape photograph.

'HOME BY THE STEPPING STONES'
Exhibited at the Photographic Society Exhibition, 1890

A young girl, in Sunday Best pinafore and straw hat, follows Granny, perhaps, across the slippery stepping stones.

ON THE MARSHES

A mixed herd of cattle, mainly shorthorns, and horses, watched over by three young minders, probably on the Essex marshes.

THE THRESHING BARN

The advent of the steam-powered threshing machine brought an end to threshing by flail. Gale noted in 1890 'The sound of the flail on the threshing-floor is as rarely heard as the note of the cuckoo in March . . .' This barn, getting rather derelict, was probably now being used for livestock.

'THE VILLAGE ALE-HOUSE'
Exhibited at the RPS House Exhibition 1901.

Refreshment at the tap-room on the way home from work, with a pint pewter tankard of the landlord's best ale. The horses are dressed with brasses for everyday working, not just for show.

A PAUSE FOR REFRESHMENT
A flat bed wagon of the type used by carriers and tradesmen, with a load of sawn timber planks. A free lunch for birds and ducks has been supplied by courtesy of the carthorse.

THE BLACKSMITH'S SHOP

The smith shoes a horse; in the background is a large grinding wheel for sharpening scythes, reaping hooks and so on. In the foreground is the platform used for putting iron hoop tyres onto wagon wheels. The wooden wheel was fixed on the platform, and the heated tyre was placed around the wheel and shrunk into place by rapid cooling with cold water.

TYRING WAGON WHEELS

Another smithy, with smoke rising from the fire used to heat the iron hoop tyres, more of which lay against the wall behind. An assistant brings in the next wheel to fit it on the platform just visible through the smoke on the right. A water container on wheels and a bucket stand on the extreme right ready for the cooling operation.

Making a Delivery

*A diminutive donkey hauls a small cart filled with sacks,
probably of coal. The prospective customer is inspecting the
quality of the goods, while in the foreground a youngster takes
a break from bowling his hoop.*

THE WOOD CART

Coppice wood cut to length for making barrel hoops, walking sticks, shepherd's crook handles and many other items, presumably on its way to the craftsman's yard.

THE CUTLER'S CART

William Terry, a travelling tradesman with his donkey cart. He would have supplied not only cutlery and scissors, but other metal goods such as penknives, needles, belts and buckles and miscellaneous trinkets.

'THE VILLAGE TRADESMAN'
Exhibited at the Photographic Society Exhibition, 1891

(Called 'The Village Jack of All Trades' in The Practical
Photographer, *1905).*
*'A quaint and characteristic figure . . . a feature of rural
England that is fast disappearing.' His 'frail' – the woven
rush shoulder basket, was used to carry his tools. His sacking
apron is an authentic part of his outfit, but the carpet
slippers he is wearing show that he was not just back from a
job, but called to pose at his front door by Gale.*

THE HEDGER AND DITCHER

*With his 'frail' for tools and lunch on his back, this character
looks the part, with his coarse but practical sacking coat,
thigh-length leather leggings and sturdy boots.*

'THE PEDLAR'

Exhibited as 'An Itinerant Dealer' in the RPS House Exhibition, 1901

Despite the spread of shops in market towns and villages during the nineteenth century, the travelling pedlar still remained remarkably common. He seems to be selling small items such as thread, needles, pins and so on.

THE BACK YARD WELL

A well right by your own back door was a luxury; most people had to share communal wells in the village street. This photograph includes a marvellous thatched beehive, with what is probably another hive next to it.

THE KNIFE GRINDER

James Clark of Sussex, with his pedal operated grindwheel mounted on a handcart. In the days before stainless steel, knives needed constant re-sharpening and polishing. The 'frail' basket would hold his tools and items for repair. He has set up close to the village well, a good place to meet prospective customers.

'A LESSON IN BASKET MAKING'
Exhibited at the Photographic Society Exhibition, 1890

Basket-making in coppice wood, probably hazel, used to make coarser but substantial basket-ware. The pupil does not seem to be paying the attention she should to her lesson!

STRAW BASKET WEAVER

The woman with the care-worn face and, presumably, her son, have returned from gleaning the cornfields for straw from which baskets, such as the one carried by the boy, can be woven. She wears a crocheted shawl, he a corduroy jacket.

A FISHING VILLAGE SCENE

All the elements one expects in a setting near the sea. The house's raised entrance, to keep the high tides out, the fisherman in knitted jersey and waterproof hat mending his nets, the barefoot lad with his shrimping net, and the waterproof hung out to dry.

BY THE SEA

Another house with a raised entrance; the thigh-length sea boots and long stockings drying on the steps show it is the home of a fisherman. The woman carries a water pitcher of the type produced by numerous small potteries around the country. The rather grumpy boy sitting by the tall nasturtium plant wears stout shoes, with knitted stockings and a jacket with a kind of caped top.

'LITTLE CHIPPERS'
Exhibited at the Photographic Society Exhibition, 1885, and
subsequently at several other shows.

*The barefoot lads have collected firewood, and presumably are
taking it around for sale. They all wear knitted jerseys, and
the location may be a fishing village.*

THE DOVECOT

An ornate dovecot, occupied by pigeons, near a watermill. The small undershot wheel shows signs of becoming overgrown, and the mill may well have stopped working. In 1890 Gale observed 'the grinding trade has gone to the towns, and has shut up the water mills to a large extent.'

'A SUSSEX MILL DAM'
Exhibited at the Salon, 1894

*A large, undershot mill wheel, driven by water passing
underneath it, with the miller sorting his fishing nets.*
The Photographic News *thought that was 'as good a
picture that this clever photographer and artist has ever
exhibited.'*

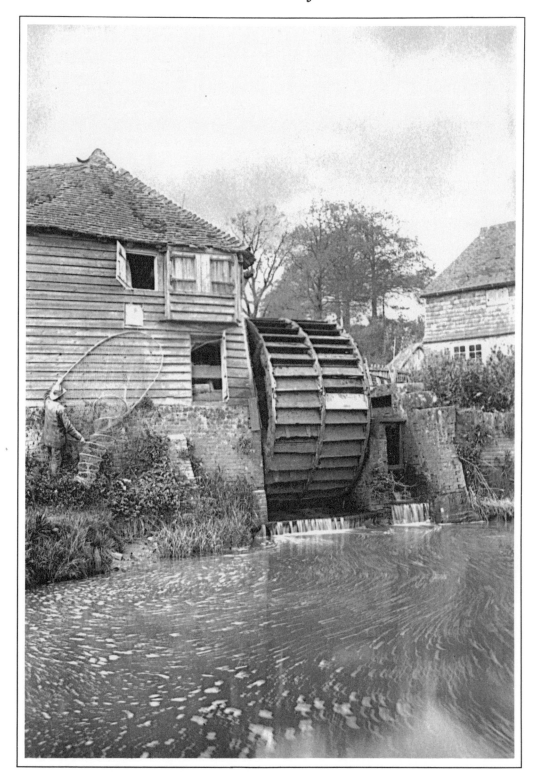

Washing Sheep

An elaborate hydraulic system for sheep washing. The washing pound is fed by two 'aqueducts'. The corner of, presumably, the sheep pen is seen on the right. The two men are wearing protective clothing made of leather pieces. The nose of a wet sheep can be seen just to the left, while another is passing through a gap in the 'dam' under the control of one of the men.

KNITTING IN THE PORCH

'With a porch at my door both for shelter and shade too,
As the sunshine or rain may prevail'
Exhibited at the Photographic Society Exhibition, 1883

An imposing setting for the old lady with her knitting. An
impressive nasturtium plant half-covers the fine porch.

'THE LACE PILLOW'

'Yon cottager who weaves at her door,
Pillow and bobbin is all her little store;
Content, tho' mean and cheerful, if not gay,
Shuffling her threads about the livelong day,
Just earns a scant pittance.' (Cowper)

Exhibited first at the Photographic Society Exhibition, 1888, and subsequently at several other shows.

Lace-making was a common occupation for labourers' wives, but was an especially important trade in Buckinghamshire and around Honiton, in Devon. The work required good light, so the woman is sitting in her doorway not just for the benefit of Gale and his camera. The bobbins were made of turned wood or bone.

A HOT LUNCH FOR FATHER

The girl is about to take a plate covered in a spotted kerchief, and carries a canister, with, perhaps, a hot drink to be delivered to someone working nearby. She wears a pinafore dress, straw hat and stout shoes for muddy roads. Note the dairy-maid's yoke by the door, the double horseshoe over the door (surely the luck is falling out?) and the neat basket on the step.

THE PUMP

Hand-pumping water was a convenient way to raise water, especially from shallow wells. Here, a water-party has arrived with a collection of containers ranging from a galvanised bucket, probably made in the Midlands, to a stoneware jug.

'THE VILLAGE WELL'

Exhibited at the RPS Exhibition, 1894, and at several other shows.

The village well was a convenient meeting place; here it is near a much adapted cottage. The general air of dereliction in many of these cottage studies gives the lie to the popular image of idyllic Victorian country life, with neat cottages and flower-filled gardens. Life in the country at the end of the last century was generally hard.

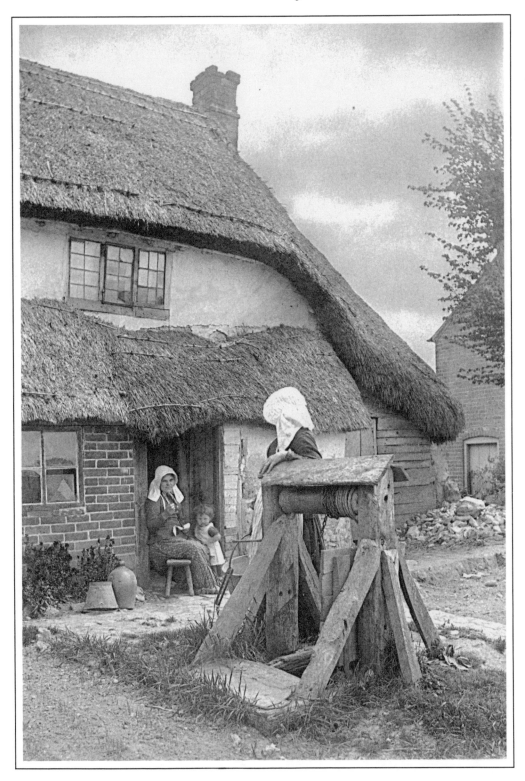

THE RAINWATER BUTT, 1888

A convenient source of water for washing was the rainwater butt by the back door. These may be servants at the farmhouse, ready to do the weekly wash.

A Water Delivery

A man wearing a yoke brings two buckets of water to the back yard. The house is a little above the labourer's cottage, and may belong to a village tradesman, or be part of a farm. The back yard is full of wheelbarrows, ladders, sieves, buckets etc. which today would have to be locked away in a shed if they were not to disappear.

'Make a walking tour of the Weald of Surrey and Sussex where suitable clay is everywhere, and each district has its brick and tile fields. See what picturesqueness can be got in the tiled roofs, with their hips, and gables, and gablets, their dormer windows and tile hangings.' Gale, 1890.

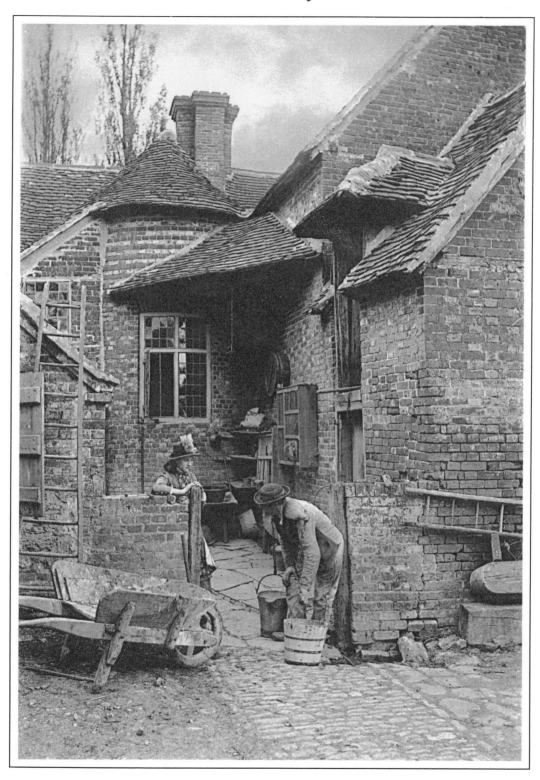

'UNDER THE VINE'

Exhibited at the Photographic Society Exhibition, 1888.

A small cottage, almost overgrown by a vine. The haggard-faced, but probably quite young, woman stands with a broom at her door, while the children play with a basket of flowers at her feet. A canary in a cage sits by the door, with a teapot hanging above (to bring it its water?). A shirt hangs drying from a small line across the window.

AT THE COTTAGE DOOR

The factory-made galvanised bucket and wire netting illustrate the steady advance of manufactured goods into the country, but the woman's birch-twig broom is thoroughly traditional. The boy wears a smart corduroy jacket and breeches. George Davison, Gale's friend and fellow photographer, was with him on this trip, and took an almost identical photograph, but with the figures in a different pose, from a camera position right next to Gale's, winning a bronze medal for it at the Oldham Photographic Exhibition in 1888, under the title 'A Cottage Home, Sussex.'

'SPINNING – A HIGHLAND DOORWAY'
Exhibited at the Photographic Society Exhibition, 1884

A croft in the Scottish Highlands, poorly constructed, with a roof covered with heather or furze. The woman wears a goffered-edged cap, plain shawl and striped apron. Notice the upturned three-legged iron cooking pot among the vessels by the door.

SPINNING

A more substantial dwelling than that in the previous example; perhaps a solid farmhouse, probably still in Scotland. The spinning wheel is slightly more elaborate; its structure is very well shown in the photograph.

A MEAL FOR THE HOP-PICKERS, 1890

Some of the army of Londoners who descended on farms in Kent for the hop-picking season. The women wear town-style hats.

PLOUGHING AND TWITCH BURNING
Exhibited at the Photographic Society Exhibition, 1893

'A skilful piece of landscape with figures; additionally interesting as showing the use of oxen with the plough.'
Ploughing with oxen continued in Sussex into the late nineteenth century. They were especially suited to the job of hauling a plough through heavy clay soils. Burning the collected twitch- (or couch-) grass was an important part of preparing the ground in the days before selective weedkillers.

AN EIGHT-OX PLOUGHING TEAM
A heavy-weight solution to ploughing on heavy Wealden clay in Sussex. The plough is a Kentish turnwrest plough, typical of the area, used for one-way ploughing. The plough is designed so that the mouldboard which turns the soil can be moved to allow ploughing across the field with all furrows turned to the same side. Without this feature, the furrows would be turned to opposite sides as the plough travelled back and forth. It looks as if the farmer has come to check the work of the ploughman and his lad.

THREE-HORSE PLOUGHING
Shown at the Camera Club one-man show, 1889.

Extra pulling power was needed for heavy soil or hilly land. The plough is a single furrow, standard iron type typical of the second half of the last century, manufactured by firms such as Howard or Ransome.

THREE-HORSE PLOUGHING

Another team at work on heavy land. This field is being ploughed in sections – 'lands' or 'stretches' – with a fixed-mouldboard plough. This ensures that furrows are in left- and right-turning groups, so as not to upset drainage. The ploughman appears to be attending to the spare team of horses, while the boss chats to a visitor at the plough. The ploughman's boy with his long whip stands smartly to attention at the horse's head.

'HOMEWARDS FROM PLOUGH'

Exhibited at the Photographic Society Exhibition, 1888; awarded two silver medals at the Richmond Photographic Exhibition, 1889 and shown at several other exhibitions over a number of years.

Ploughing teams on their way home, in the Berkshire uplands. Another occasion when George Davison was present; his photograph, taken from the opposite direction, was also much exhibited.

'Mr. Gale . . . has secured an excellent picture full of life, and yet he has caught in it the lazy, workdone sort of movement of the horses.' Amateur Photographer.

PLOUGHMAN'S LUNCH

The real thing; flagons of beer or cider were often supplied by the farmer. The young man by the horses' heads, with leather gaiters and what may be velveteen trousers, is smoking a fancy pipe with a silver band. His seated companion is also quite smartly dressed for the field. The two older men wear more traditional garb.

A BREAK FROM HARROWING

Harrowing was usually a spring-time operation, done to break down the ploughed land after the winter frosts, and then repeated after sowing to rake over the soil. The harrow is made from flexible iron links rather like chain fencing. A spare harrow lies on the bank behind the workmen. The horses have their nose-bags on, while the seated workman has a bottle of liquid refreshment with a head on it.

'A HOLLOW OF THE DOWNS'
Illustrated in *Practical Photographer* 1903.

*Rolling the ploughed land in the spring to prepare a seed-bed.
Three horses were needed for this heavy job on rising land.*

'POTATO PLANTING, NOVEMBER'
Shown in the Crystal Palace Exhibition, 1898 and the RPS
House Exhibition, 1901.

*A simple plough turns a furrow, and a team of men and
women plant the potatoes. It was backbreaking work, carrying
heavy baskets and bent double over the soil.*

THE HAYFIELD

'Bow' wagons, typical of the time, with a box body, side rails to allow loads to overhang, and 'ladders' – uprights at the front and back. The hay, collected using wide wooden hay rakes, is loaded with pitch-forks.

HAYMAKING

Open parkland, with a team of men and women resting from their work with broad wooden hay rakes.

'OAT CUTTING IN SUSSEX'
Exhibited at the Photographic Society Exhibition, 1887

Hand cutting with bagging hooks. The women gather up and tie the sheaves, while the old chap sets up the stooks. 'The alterations in the game laws have probably brought about the disuse of the sickle throughout the land.' Gale, 1890.

CORN CUTTING BY MACHINE
The corn is cut here with a hay mower, leaving a continuous swathe which had to be gathered into bundles by hand, a job that the youngsters could help with.

WHEAT HARVESTING BY SAIL REAPER

A scene redolent of warm summer days. The children wait to stack the sheaves, bound by the man, into stooks.

CORN HARVESTING WITH A BINDER

A self-binding reaper which cut the corn, and passed it over belts on the right-hand side to be tied automatically. These machines were introduced progressively from the 1890s, and remained in universal use until the arrival of the combine harvester. This photograph illustrates the mixed corn and sheep husbandry which has been lost from the light-soiled downlands since 1941.

'THE SHEPHERD AND HIS BOY'
Exhibited at the Crystal Palace Exhibition, 1898 and at the RPS
House Exhibition in 1901.

*The lad is wearing a smock, which by the 1890s had largely
gone out of common usage. Notice the neatly thatched corn
ricks in the field.*

'NINETY-AND-NINE'
Exhibited at the Photographic Society Exhibition, 1890.

The shepherd with the strayed lamb; well protected against the winds of the open country with jerkin and thick woollen jumper.

THE YOUNG SHEPHERD AND HIS DOG

An alert dog, with his young master wearing the waterproof jacket, rather like a modern anorak, which had replaced the traditional smock by the end of the century.

'THE MONK'S WALK AT CHENIES'
Exhibited at the Photographic Society Exhibition, 1889

A characteristic study by Gale of one of his favourite subjects, sheep. Reviewing the exhibition, The Photographic News *said of Gale's pictures '. . . they are types of delicacy, admirable balance and manipulative skill . . . Over Mr. Gale's sheep in "The Monk's Walk at Chenies" Mr. Sydney Cooper would go into raptures.'*

SHEEP ON THE DOWNS
A striking composition, with the flock of sheep in the foreground set against the massive chalk quarrying operations in the distance. Not much can be left by now of the hillside.

SHEEP ON THE HILLSIDE

'Even with cattle in the field, or sheep on the hills, ease of manner will greatly assist in getting on photographically friendly terms with them . . . make up your mind from a distance as to your best point of view. Avoid going straight for them or looking straight at them. If using a stand camera, set it up so that it may be seen at a distance, and not sprung upon them suddenly. Approach them quietly, wandering hither and thither . . .' Gale, 1905.